X121203848   BLK

The Blues Cry For A Revolution

Rashaun J. Allen

Poems that give voice to revolution

Dallas Public Library

Royal Blue Publishing | New York City

Copyright © 2019 by **Rashaun J. Allen**

All rights reserved. No part of this publication may be reproduced, distributed or transmitted in any form or by any means, without prior written permission.

Rashaun J. Allen/Royal Blue Publishing
www.rashaunjallen.com

Publisher's Note: This is a work of fiction. Names, characters, places, and incidents are a product of the author's imagination. Locales and public names are sometimes used for atmospheric purposes. Any resemblance to actual people, living or dead, or to businesses, companies, events, institutions, or locales is completely coincidental.

Book Layout © 2019 BookDesignTemplates.com

Bronx Tree cover and back art by © 2019 Justin Bua

Library of Congress Control Number: 2019914149

The Blues Cry for a Revolution/ Rashaun J. Allen. -- 1st ed.
ISBN 978-0-98300967-2 (Paperback)
ISBN 978-0-98300968-9 (Kindle)
ISBN 978-0-98300969-6 (Epub)

Dedicated to the unknown victims of injustice.

Also by Rashaun J. Allen

A Walk Through Brooklyn
In The Moment

Contents

I. For The Unknown Victims

"Miracles happen all the time. We're here, aren't we?"

— *Marilyn Nelson*

Brevity of a Black Boy

Black face—
your mask is your skin.
Cops will shoot you and claim you ignited suspicion.

Black legs—
wherever you walk in sneakers or shoes
you're step-down to a second-class citizen.

Black hands—
enter that store and touch nothing
still, you're followed like a shadow.

Black body—
a menace to society
know that a prison cell was built for you.

Black mind—
think carefully
you expect life, liberty, and justice?

Black life—
compressed 'til death
this is what us, black boys, call "Everyday living."

When Barbershops Are Empty

There are no GOAT conversations
or big screens displaying playoff games
Nor neck turns with step show precision
when fine black women crisscross our vision.

There are no great debates of back in my day,
nobody who was somebody allowed shit to happen to anyone.
From Knubia Kutts to any numbered street in Canarsie
5 Percenters would break down mathematics of poverty.
Politics would cross paths with blackness
like those customers who came in selling you whatever you didn't
need.

When barbershops are empty
there's no scramble for seats
those 2 hours waiting are no more.
I hop right in the barber's chair,
waves, frohawk, or a low fade
and don't forget to connect the beard.
"Where are our brothers?" a sister asks 'round the same time my
barber spins the chair.

She's craving a strong, educated, black man who stands on his
convictions.
But who she describes is so rare the media claims he's fiction:
more are incarcerated, less finish college
and every day our deaths don't add up.
When barbershops are empty there ain't no black men here.

Just Another

The trigger's pulled and I'm lifeless.

Aim, shoot, squeeze decisive. The outer layer of my cerebrum holding on...

Misunderstood. Misconstrued. Motionless.

The cure for cancer spilling out my mind.

Several emptied clips. Confiscated recordings. The story he ain't shit.

All I needed was a safe space to thrive.
All I needed was a safe space to thrive.
All I needed was a safe space to thrive.

Instead, my hands up, fresh cut, pants buckled, no hoodie, proper speech, both parents, honor roll, church goer, big brother, working man, community servant, and patriot, "I am still gunned down!"

Ten Reasons

I am killed:
Carrying a fake gun [1]
Selling CDs[2]
Routine traffic stops [3]
Improper lane change [4]
A broken tail light [5]
Holding a wallet[6]
Waiting for roadside assistance[7]
Walking[8]
Sleeping[9]
Breathing.[10]

---

[1] Tamir Rice
[2] Alton Sterling
[3] Samuel DuBose
[4] Sandra Bland
[5] Philando Castile
[6] Amadou Diallo
[7] Corey Jones
[8] Michael Brown
[9] Aiyana Stanley-Jones
[10] Eric Garner

Ain't a Black Holiday

How can I celebrate the Fourth of July?
When racism is as American as burgers and fries.
The declaration of independence's ink dried up
without a word freeing enslaved Africans
black murdered bodies spilled Mississippi River length blood
from then 'till now.
Don't wish me a "Happy holiday!"
Ain't nothing holy 'bout countless lives lost.
Find a time in U.S. history when black and brown people didn't
experience a black holocaust.
Any position we hold is jubilantly broadcasted as a post racial face list
but below the surface systematic oppression still exists.
I'm way passed angry, pissed, and furious.
Anytime we take a knee the response is a well packaged shut-the-
hell-up.
This beautiful nation has been around for over 240 years
that's over ten generations of us being treated less than
a love for the only country we call home doesn't mean accept fool's
gold.
Reparations, twenty acres, a mule, and re-opening all criminal cases
where racial bias is proved
would be some goals to undo some of the injustice accrued.

A Stolen People

We, a stolen people, live, and die on stolen land
land stolen, we, a stolen people, die without living
living without dying, we, a stolen people, have invisible dreams
dreams invisible, we, a stolen people, struggle to imagine
imagine, we, a stolen people, were people.

For Brown Girls Whose Names Never Amber Alert

On my Facebook news feed, I unsee, "Black Girls Missing."
a black girl, now just black.
I unhang up the video chat with my sister.
She untells me about her day.
I take back my advice
"Makers trouble ignore."
She unlaughs, they don't know who she is.
I undecided to say what I didn't follow at sixteen.
Unwalk inside my apartment
to unshow her the proximity of New Jersey stores
the bus stop, the diner, the park.
I unlost the words to say
I love you and I care.
They uncame out as wherever I am you're welcome here.
The brief silence unechoed the states between us.
She unasked me what I was doing.
I unwatched her grow from a young lady to a girl.
I forgot her smile shines in a dark room.
Her name unslip from my tongue.
Her face I could no longer see.
She's no longer in the family pictures.
But she's closer than my skin to me.
My skin unattached to my body.
My body unreceives oxygen.
Missing never felt like death
'til a life is taken from you
while you're both still breathing.

For the Unknown
Victims of Systematic Oppression

I can't wrap my durag around this do bad.
Like doing twenty years of hard time and you're innocent.
You in your home screaming, "It's a nightmare!"
You wake up the CO is right there.
No hashtag, no protest
just

                          dank

               bars

                    and visits.

No lawyer fees
just

        the

               judge

                      and in your case there ain't been no
               locomotion in your disposition.
Your hypothesis, a synonym
for rubbish, gibberish, hogwash, and nonsense.
The world is numb to your murmur.
Real shit!
You been strong so long you   strung out   on it.
A good palliative of family support
                 that never made it.
Regardless of the time
you got plans to see the sun, right?
Your son, right?
He's getting bigger too.
The world doesn't peep his   genius.
To them   he's nothing.
You do everything to survive.

II. For Those Who Watch

"Poetry is a political act because it involves telling the truth"

— *June Jordan*

Prose to the Silent Conscious Man

I.   I don't know how to reach you, since when you speak in person or through social media, you are aware of current events.

II.   I see you in every man who goes to work and comes home to watch sports until you're asked a direct question, "What do you think about the systematic incarceration of black and brown people who are locked up disproportionately to white people despite committing crimes at similar rates?"

III.   My granddad, father, uncles, cousins, and myself have been placed in handcuffs, I want to tell you, while I write my days away.

IV.   The more I write the more I discover our narrative was meant to be forgotten.

V.   "Because my father didn't bond with his Dad," my conscious screams, "it's okay to repeat family history."

VI.   "Nor does my family share memories," I write in my journal reflecting over the silence that filled my granddad's room when asked about his childhood.

VII.

VIII.   There was a loose paper left by my Great-Grandma, my Granddad's Mom. It held names and places of people who were kin to me but strangers at the same time.

IX.   You are like Wi-Fi.

X.   When I want to connect, you are not in service for black lives.

XI.   (A survival tactic, I'm sure.)

XII.   I need to learn how we can thrive without you.

XIII.   And still be open to you when you're ready.

XIV.   As if you're a branch from my family tree.

For Black Cops Who Bleed Blue

The NYPD's salary and benefits offers optional retirement at one half
salary after 22 years of service. In that time frame, our community
will suffer more unreasonable arrests multiplied by time served and it
still won't equal one unjustified death.

I respect your position and understand your crisis filled work weeks
still might not be enough to pay for your child's college tuition. But
your quiet is deafening.

You stand behind the blue wall of silence.
You want to shake the system from inside.
But outside you have to careen justice even alone.

How else do you expect citizens to respect cops?
We not hearing, "You don't know what it's like to wear a badge."
That profession is chosen from first breath we black.

We're not mad at you just calling a slave a slave.
They treat us like runaways.
Don't look away as radio waves scan for black bodies.

Black bodies should not be criminalized
shot dead no matter their juxtaposition.
Egregious intuition transforming into judge, jury, and sentence.

Protect us
serve the community that loved you
before your skin turned blue.

A Home Nowhere

He had a sleeping bag full of his belongings—some rags and coins that made up his riches. He held a sign that read, "I'm homeless and need a little help." But he didn't say a word, silence held his vocal cords hostage as he watched feet scramble on the concrete block. I heard someone utter, "What's stopping him from working like us?"

I heard his story before. He had a modest dream to become a firefighter. But after 9/11 he felt compelled to take his patriotism one step further. His pride beamed from his heart to his head the first day he wore his army fatigues. Yet after seeing agony his life grew slanted. He never forgot the day he watched a kid blow up. A drone used intelligence and landed a precise strike.

Two years later his wife left and took everything but his dog he called "Liberty."

It took me a New-York-minute to figure out he had no idea the last time he was sober. I started to feel bad. I reached in my pocket for change. As if my small action could do more than a political campaign. I happened to see my watch. It was a quarter to nine. I was running late and my boss was already tired of my poor timing. I shook my head empty-handed and blended right back in with the crowd full of excuses.

Bench Player

I heard, "Retail workers who want better wagers are entitled."
Full-time at fifteen is about $31,000 dollars
in New York City, that's not even survival.
I'm no Malcolm X, nor MLK
but when bills come faster than paychecks
marching on days off ain't happening.
I toe the line between surviving and dying.

I got a college degree
thinking, *the world would be full of opportunity*
and went from unemployed to under-employed.
With student debt rising,
I can barely afford where I live.
No cable.
My prize possessions: an Iphone, a ten-year-old car and a whole lot
of ambition.
I wonder, everyday how to change my position.

I count my blessing yet I skip tithe.
It's safe in these church walls
but what am I to do when I'm outside?
I'm financially stuck being a bench player
rooting for the good guys while the bad guys laugh.

Bystander

In the suite, a baseball game took place.
A friend went to bat for a woman, we both knew. The chase around
the field happened fast-ball-quick. Inside a room, a homerun was hit.
Like exchanging gloves, the players switched. Another never touched
base and stole what was never pitched.

Take me out of this ball game.
Take me out of this crowd.
Pour me a drink and blast the music
I don't think this scene I'll ever forget.
If it's root, root, root for the home team
what I just seen is a shame.

Graffiti

He could be an athlete, a dog, a star. But growing up in the summer responding to life is deadly. There's a double consciousness in his head. Many will write off his ability as a follower with no future. But can't a rose bloom through concrete? He changes his C's to B's and offers us (on Twitter) his bonundrum. *Thank God for life. But I'll send anybody to hell.* There's a glance of unfuckwitable pride— surely, he learned it from a bousin. He wants love (but the streets are undefeated) and he drifts away, a bapital seventh letter, unbothered, his splattered brains will be a rival's street art.

Future Self

Who would read my eulogy?
I hope it's someone so close to me
their heart skipped a beat when mine stopped.
She would step upon the podium with no tears and shout
not for nothing this brother, husband, father, and son
led a life with no fears.
Thank you for coming, I know he's watching
and he'll get a kick out of hearing his story.
A Momma's boy who lost his Momma at fourteen
adopted by his granddad, he ran towards the streets.
He went to school but chased the cool
until he played a fool.
Found his dream at college,
fell in love with knowledge,
went from surviving to thriving.
His own business, books, and Netflix deals,
held his family close to his heart,
until the day his heartbeat stopped.
Dear future self,
five, ten, twenty years from now,
will you look back fulfilled?

Piano Keys

My dream: a Shadd Piano inside my living room.
My fingers: play, "Strange Fruit."
My guests: sing along.
My hope: this lived ambition enhances our collective position.
And overwhelming black-boy-joy covers my scars.
Despite images ingrained of black lives
no longer lynched from trees
but falling from bullets in the streets.

A Spaceship Named Respect

Sometimes I want to fly away in a spaceship
leave for mars on the first flight out of JFK
where my chance of respect is greater
this warrior's heart is beat
too tired to fight, fight, fight
the devilish details derail my sanity.
What else did you expect from me?
Black
a beautiful detail of my being
I
fight to overcome a Mount Everest of problems
from
sunrise to sunset
the further I push against the ceiling
the more malleable it becomes
the harder it gets
the more I wish to fly
this hell has no bottom
maybe heaven is outside of earth
an alien race can't do anything
my blackness hasn't faced.

Unequal

privilege

                passes down to each generation

                                    hardship too.

                We wake up

                and

              work, work, work.

Still there are few: black teachers, lawyers, and doctors

            and many: white managers, CEOs, and investors

            success passes around us.

Them: hard-work and innate genius

                        us: luck and affirmative action

      lies have besieged our vision.

        Sometimes the poor are white and the rich are black.

          Sometimes the natives are forgotten

          Like the foreignness' of our past.

    Sometimes the audacity of hope ain't enough for change.

But none of that explains, why hasn't the American Dream found us?

Signs Your World Will End

I.   A homeless man will be offered a place to stay.

II.   Justice will be affordable to the poor.

III.   A country founded by immigrants will welcome immigrants.

IV.   The strings attached to education will not be debt.

V.   Mainstream media will no longer hold journalism hostage.

VI.   Your difference will not start a checklist of hate.

VII.   You'll step out your comfort zone and make a friend that doesn't look like you.

VIII.   Facts will overstand fear.

IX.   Your character will be the only brand that matters.

X.   History won't repeat itself.

III. For Those Who Resist

"Not everything that is faced can be changed, but nothing can be changed until it is faced."

— *James Baldwin*

Good Ass System

Somebody somewhere is saying, "We got a good ass system."
We could change all the laws and still get 'em,
we can box 'em in so many wrongs; right won't fit 'em.
Discrimination ain't like my Granddad days
but I swear there's a sign up that reads, "No Colored Allowed To
Breathe."
Stereotypes are more common than cursive.
Books are contraband in jails like black bodies are purses.
Highlight black lives matters
somebody somewhere is saying, "All lives matter, you ass hole."
As if you could tell me how to feel,
as if working twice as hard is a deal,
as if being young, black, and conscious is too real.
Good Lord, I can't comprehend this frustration
seeing aunts, uncles, brothers, and sisters killed like the Walking
Dead.
Instead of praised like Scientists, Engineers, someone with creativity.
I wish a negro spiritual could free us at last.
But truth be told between the world and me
I declare war on this hypocrisy.

1,000 Days

Kalief Browder's *suicide* hurt me.
He did three years with no trial.
Nearly 1,000 days locked up off a whim.
Identified to a crime he never was proven linked to.
His family couldn't afford a lawyer
Imagine explaining your story ten, no, hundreds of times just for
people not to believe you.
At some point, it may mess with your logic.
The constant pressure he felt to plead guilty just to escape cold steel
bars.
COs despised him.
Others saw him as a target, locked in, and took shot after shot at him.
He wasn't ready for that kind of life.
No one is but as far as we know Kalief was just a 16-year-old high
school kid.
Until his life became a nightmare, he felt he couldn't escape.
It doesn't matter that Kalief was released from Riker's island.
Could he press rewind on 1,000 days?
Could he put on a suit and people not think he belongs in a cage?
That young man was left enraged.
Afraid
      anything given
           was just
                 staged.
He understood too well how things were given—freedom, liberty,
and just us left somewhere between probation and a lengthy
sentence.
For all I know, I'm Kalief Browder, the only difference I returned
home the same day from a stop and frisk.
So when you say Kalief Browder committed suicide.
I want you to understand I don't condone suicide.
But he felt like it was his only choice.
It was him being brave.

Black Boy Joy

For Travon Martin

You ain't supposed to smile black boy

    for those who look like us are behind cold steel bars.

You ain't supposed to cry black boy

    for too many of us never get to grow old.

You ain't supposed to live for the future

    'cause your daddy left you somewhere in the past.

You ain't supposed to laugh black boy

       unless the jokes on you,
         on your skin,
         on your vision.

     How could you fly with clipped wings?

Fly through bullets,

    fly through hate,

       fly through fear?

You ain't supposed to   soar   black   boy.

You find black boy joy in your dance.
Stompin' the yard
ain't no half steppin' along the way.

     You find black boy joy in your style.
The way your kicks complement your shirt I tip my hat you got black
        boy swag.

You are not the exception. Accept the excellence your brown skin illuminates.
You too can be a doctor, a scholar, a writer.

Don't crack black boy. Don't lean black boy. You may fall but get up by any means black boy.

You are not a hater.
You are a brother, a husband, a father.
You're a born winner in this cold, cold, world.
Grow and glow like your afro black boy.

You are Lebron James, Jay-Z, Denzel Washington.
You are Diddy. You are Will Smith.
You are a dream so big.
You are a diamond so bright.
You are surviving.
You are thriving.
Be brilliant. Be brotherly. Be brave.
Black boy your mind is a canvas; your actions a brush.
Black boy brilliance I see a black boy being crowned king.

You are black boy joy!

Between Fists Lies Unwavering Rage

Street fight
black versus white
outsiders gamble upon a life.

Their adrenaline rushing
blood boiling
as spectators glide through life—

Fair shot—
lost between moments of
before and after,
fair shot—
lost between moments of
survival and death,
fair shot—
lost between moments of
far-fetched bruising
traveling generations of grayed realities
incubate a destiny not yet formed
words not yet discovered
to articulate a desire that goes beyond giving the world all you got.

To square up on life
get ready for the impossible
surrounded by a foreign destiny
send that hook shot hard enough to be heard round the world,
knocking down any opposition.

23 Hours

Isolation. Segregation. Special Management and Restricted Housing all lead to a bed, a toilet, a shower, and a slot large enough for a guard to slip a food tray through. But the slot is not large enough to show what solitary confinement does to a mind.

23 hours a day. 730 hours a month. 8,766 hours in a year. I'm off by a couple of hours. But all it took was the McGill University students less than a week to lose the ability to think clearly about anything for any length of time.

Have you ever heard a survivor speak? About the fear that swells up from being constantly alone. About waking up consumed in sweat in the fetal position? About hurting their own flesh to sense how reality feels?

Would you call access to television, craft books, and magazines a prisoner's dream? The exercise yard—that small area fenced in concrete, too freeing? The UN has called for solitary confinement to be banned as a form of torture—would you agree?

Any state sanction act, "By which severe pain of suffering whether physical or mental that is intentionally inflicted on a person is torture." For what—violating prison rules? A system reclassification that has nothing to do with behavior? What good comes out of extreme isolation?

There are more than 80,000 American prisoners being held in isolation from convicted felons to political prisoners.[11] Some prisoners spent more than a decade without family visits.
And to those who do have visits a glass screen guarantees non-contact. If you had the power would you amend this ordeal?

---

[11] American Friends Service Committee. "Solitary Confinement Facts." https://www.afsc.org/resource/solitary-confinement-facts#.

Young Radical Mind

Reimagine a different world
where black lives matter
wars are obsolete
immigrants are welcomed
self-knowledge is more popular than a selfie
white privilege is checked like ID
beauty standards reflect
you, him, her, and they
dog whistle politics are fought against like terrorists
minimum wage is a livable wage
actors are politicians
leaders actually take the stage
ESPN covers teachers like athletes
paying for education is a crime
jails are not pipelines
but life lines to help the incarcerated
police are from the community
where a village raises a child
to go to Marcus Garvey University
reimagine a better life
one step at a time
reimagine a better life
young radical mind
reimagine a better life
a new world within reach
reimagine
you make this life a reality.

Language is a Color Now

Let these words sound tight or forever sound white
Agitated by closed minds refusing to self-express
Notorious nonsense no gaze should come before we, us, and our
Gentrified black bodies we no longer need massa to whip us
Understand this war on melanin began before we existed
Amplified by social media you can't log out of ignorance
Gravitate towards a like mind and end up alone

Institutions have racism sewed into its fabric
Systems only fall when the oppressed stand up

A explanation can never turn a wrong right

Casual colorism is rampant amongst my peers and I
Out of this world thoughts are justified logically
Language is meant to communicate but no one is listening
Opinions should hold less weight than facts
Rage fills each poem expressed

No answers will appear without action
Obvious oppression is laughed off
What are we waiting for?

Game from a Young Me

Remember rumors spread like wildfires
while truth blooms like a flower.
Never be scared to try your luck.
The ruckus is where the magic happens.
Can your fortitude be broken?
Don't use words when actions shout.
You'll thank me later
and habits last a lifetime.
The will comes before the skill
and don't go extinct like the pterosaur.
Only go after a goal when your heart is in it
and only if your heart is prepared to fail.
Victory is kin to you like blood
when doubters spew nothing but fear.
If you can't handle storm in your life
there's no way you'll be the future me.

Unwavering

I.
No need to question
my situation I am
destined for greatness.

II.
Deep rooted diamonds
shine through relentless pressure
fear leaves the body.

III.
The path paved is filled
with concrete perseverance
against oppression.

Stop

Hands up. Holding nothing but air in a space not inclusive—I can't breathe. Bland faces can't discern the catastrophe that is my reality. A conundrum. Who would you feed first, a murderer of nine parishioners in Charleston or a homeless man on 8th Avenue? Instead, the answer is incoherent. No time lost in the peripheral vision of a demonic world high off testosterone. Burnt at the stake for telling the truth. "Despicable," they shouted. All I wanted was to point out the oligarchy. All they wanted was mimosas to drink. The coming of my funeral left me ineffable. Just know I didn't waste my inquisitive mind.

I've Come Too Far

over trials and tribulations
to let your bullshit
disrupt my situation.

I've come too far
to give up on a dream
not yet fulfilled.

I've come too far
worked twice as hard
to get half the distance
just for you to think I need your permission.

I've come too far
fell and failed on my way here
to stop pushing further
until my last breath.

I've come too far
lost family I thought I couldn't live without
to think any problem, I'm faced with
I can't figure out.

Unbought, uncompromising
you understand
cut off my right hand; I'll learn to write with my left.

The only thing
I'll ever accept
is my best.

Racism is a Thing

Too many more times than I can articulate, I've thought about knuckling up against racism. But I couldn't determine whether racism was a person, place, or thing. Something I could hold then crush. Or an idea too big to obliterate.

Either way, I believe I'd end up with too much racism. I joked if this enemy fought me fair, the odds would change based on the setting.

But if I was able to choke racism then stomp it out like a fly, wouldn't that break the internet? I've got the feeling I'd be playing a team sport—alone.

In that case, I'd have to visualize myself—larger than my life—a symbol that rings for generations.

A Concrete Garden

They tried to bury us
smothered in concrete
dreams splattered on project walls
sunlight piercing the netherworld—
joy, hard-work, and a future worth living dismissed as hocus pocus.

Round here every day a dry season
knowledge a food desert
watered with miseducation
severe suffering
raked too many into mischief.

In Brooklyn,
glass ceilings won't let visions sprout
priced out of what is already unaffordable
planted gentrifiers foresee another Starbucks
where chop cheese sells
fire hydrants burst but the screams we never hear yell.

They tried to bury us—
redirect our pain to a fourth dimension. Somehow our three-
dimensional lives are too deep to be understood by one nation under
God.

They tried to bury us—
wash away our history from and kinship to west Africa. Confine our
story to a period: enslavement then incarceration.

They tried to bury us—
by showing us those who disproved our truth. One success story is
not enough to make countless others invisible.

But they forgot we were seeds.
Planted by the green thumbs of our mothers
rich in nutrients, we turn tragedy to protein
muscle our roots into worldwide trends
buried generations deep
still we rise like Maya
against all odds like Pac.
Imagine the spoils if the soil was even?
Twice as good cracking through concrete
We sprout wherever we are planted.

Dream While Woke

My dream is
closer than a millennial to technology
closer than a lady to her purse
closer than an artery.

Failure is
not in my vocabulary
unauthorized in my repertoire
a disrespect to my skillset.

The color of my skin nor my net worth will stop me.
Words bursting through 10,000 sleepless nights
so hungry
my food
the fruit from my labor.

A Melody on Repeat

Peek into my rebirth.
Cramped,
elevator music is spinning in my mind
I am
        inspired by syncopated rhythms
digging
        fiendishly for a gold standard vision
neither in the past or present
but an outer body experience in another dimension,
tapping inspiration into submission—
What words to produce?
That ring true to my core,
spread over a world wide web
that can tell the story of my plight.
Miscellaneous cues are worthy.
Stagnating frequency.
Vibe with me
outside a box that trapped your genius.
All great artists were once called mad.
Outside the flames of a phoenix
is no other than my life's work.

Speaking Hennessy

Liar, liar, liar
said the croc to the king of the jungle
Then why he's fighting?
His point of view surviving
transforming deception to ambition.
Eyes on fire to torch any superstition
that black boys don't fly like Michael Jordan,
that black girls ain't magic, not Houdini
but Serena, Beyoncé, Queen Sheba.

Liar, liar, liar
said the land of the free and home of the brave.
Then how my brothers locked up while y'all so afraid?
Your point of view of us—super predators.
Transforming descendants of enslaved to 13th amendment made
criminals.
But what shall we call inheritors of stolen land, stolen bodies, stolen
wealth: blood spillers, curse folk—wicked demons.
Can't stop my spider sense from tingling,
this deception is vaster than the seven seas.

Liar, liar, liar
said hard-work leads to a good job.
But how is working for the man your only dream?
My point of view is leave a legacy
creating hoods like Black Wall Street.
So, in this different world
caged birds don't only sing,
"We gon' be alright."
But soar through the impossible.

Dear I

I know it's hard out here in this ocean
where everyone's a shark trying to eat.
Blood dripping, your feet numb tired of kicking
face up against the current drowning.
Who knew, swim, breath, meddle through oxygen
optionless the hypothesis, "Don't you quit."
Shine brighter than any battleship
from miles to yards, push through
until your feet find land
toes on soil, no date can spoil this moment.
Look beyond your blues
and let your heart's rhythm show the way.
You are destined for greatness
ever since leaving the shallow waters of fear.

Invisible Man

Have you ever been in a room full of strangers? Where everybody knows your name but no one knows your pain. It's nothing they want to see. Even if it showed up on TV, a Facebook newsfeed, or in a piece of poetry. You're screaming but only quiet comes across.

What if I told you police killed at least 378 people since Kaepernick took a knee?[12] Would you take a knee?

What if I told you police have killed at least 2,902 people since Ferguson?[13] Would you think I hate police?

The difference between white America and black America is when an unarmed black man or woman is killed by police; black America knows it can be us, white America changes the channel,

Click, click, "Let's watch *Keeping Up with the Kardashians*."

I'm tired of talking about systematic oppression. I see it how I am treated. I inhale it while you raise your nose to it. Your words spoken about it are horror to my ears. The mere idea of justice is met with warlike resistance. I conclude, you not getting it is a choice.

There's no time in history where an oppressor told the oppressed it is over. It's always a fight. It always leaves too many incapacitated to hear what is said by an invisible man.

---

[12] Murdock, Sebastian. "Police Killed at Least 378 Black Americans from The Moment Colin Kaepernick Protest." Huffington Post, May 24th, 2018. https://www.huffingtonpost.com/entry/police-killed-378-black-americans-colin-kaepernick_us_5b070160e4b07c4ea10655be.
[13] Lopez, German; Oh, Soo. May 17th, 2017 "Police have shot and killed at least 2,902 people since Ferguson." Vox, https://www.vox.com/a/police-shootings-ferguson-map.

Black Spaces

For us in America

A place we call home that's not broken
or redlined rarely exists
from watching our backs to warding off mental attacks.
Where is the black space to flourish?

Where every difference isn't a dividing factor
our problems matter
in a culture that protects you, me, him, and her.
Am I out of place?

A place to sleep
ain't the same as a place to live
a place to praise, a place to raise our kids.
Where is the black space to raise out of the everyday struggle?

Our home is here:
however, we create
a place between the hood and a mansion
where our space is defined by us.

What Should I call It?

For those buried in the African Burial Grounds

Maybe this poem should be titled, "I got you"
'cause when I saw the African Burial Ground in New York City I swore
I wouldn't forget you.
Or
Maybe this poem should be titled, "Pissed"
'cause how many times could I see descriptions like, "96 young men
between sixteen and eighteen years old buried here" and pretend
the days of being treated like shit are over.
Or
Maybe this poem should be titled, "Hope"
'cause they better pray we don't pull a Nat Turner and go out with a
bang.
Or
Maybe this poem should be titled, "Unwavering"
For us to live through horror for generations is greater than any
world wonder.
Or
Maybe this poem should be titled, "Lucky"
seeing a mass grave, I'm reminded that I'm one bad day, no, one
moment in time from being buried with them.
Or
Maybe this poem should be called, "Woke"
'Cause after speaking to my ancestors, I will never sleep under
oppression again.

Blaxplosion

7
generations
of black rage
pinned up in a
black-body-grenade
the fuse is shorter
than lady liberty's memory
of my stolen, raped, and enslaved ancestors
alternate facts
won't mute the explosion.

Acknowledgements

I am grateful to these publications who published earlier forms of the following poems: "A Melody on Repeat" in *Poui*, No: XVIII, "Game from a Young Me" in *Auburn Avenue*, Autumn/Winter, Issue III, "Prose to the Silent Conscious Man" and "A Spaceship Named Respect" in *Hypertext* Spring 2019, volume 4.

I am thankful to the Vermont Studio Center for providing me with the time and space to write. Justin Bua, the artist, who allowed me to use his Bronx Tree artwork for the cover and back. My partner, Rosaura Elías-Wilson, for her unwavering support. Jordan Franklin and Julissa Thompson for their edits with this collection of poems.

I want to recognize the many poets who inspired my work: Mahogany L. Browne, Danez Smith, Safia Elhillo, Tammy Lopez, Afua Ansong, Claudia Rankine, Terrance Hayes, Jacqueline Woodson, Vievee Francis and Nate Marshall.

Still, I can't forget my teachers and mentors: Terese Svoboda and Star Black. My old and new friends, line brothers and Phi Beta Sigma Fraternity Inc. and my whole family for all the love and backing.

Finally, you who decided to endorse my art. Thank you.

Rashaun J. Allen is a writer, entrepreneur, poet, professor, and a Fulbright recipient. A past Vermont Studio Center and Arts Letters & Numbers resident whose two poetry chapbooks: *A Walk Through Brooklyn* and *In The Moment* became Amazon Kindle Best Sellers. He has been nominated for Sundress Publication's 2018 Best of the Net Anthology in Creative Non-Fiction and was a 2017 Steinberg Essay Contest Finalist in *Fourth Genre*. You can visit his website rashaunjallen.com for more of his work.

CPSIA information can be obtained
at www.ICGtesting.com
Printed in the USA
LVHW031602040220
645814LV00003B/600

9 780983 009672